Tra

POEMS

WORKS BY STEVEN SMITH

Transient Light
The Mercury Press (an imprint of Aya Press), 1990

Sleepwalkers (with Richard Truhlar) (book & audiocassette)
Underwhich Editions, 1987

blind zone Aya Press, 1985

Sign Language (with Owen Sound) (audiocassette)
Underwhich Editions, 1985

Ritual Murders Turnstone Press, 1983

Between, Sequence 3 (with jwcurry)
Phenomenon Press and Curvd H&Z, 1982

Three Naturals Underwhich Editions, 1980

Transient Light

POEMS

Steven Smith

for Brooke.

Steven Smith
1991

The Mercury Press
(an imprint of Aya Press)
Stratford, Ontario

The publisher gratefully acknowledges
the financial assistance of the Canada Council
and the Ontario Arts Council.
The publisher further acknowledges the financial assistance of the
Saskatchewan Arts Board in the publication of this volume,
with thanks.

Cover photograph by André Kertész.
Collection of the Jane Corkin Gallery.
Used by permission and with thanks.
Editor for the press: Beverley Daurio
Production co-ordination: The Blue Pencil
Printed and bound in an edition of 750 copies at
The Coach House Press, Toronto, Canada.

....

Sales Representation: The Literary Press Group.
The Mercury Press is distributed in Canada
by University of Toronto Press, and in the United States
by Inland Book Company (selected titles)
and Bookslinger.

THE MERCURY PRESS
(an imprint of Aya Press)
Box 446, Stratford, Ontario
Canada N5A 6T3

Canadian Cataloguing in Publication

Smith, Steven, 1945 -
Transient light

ISBN 0-920544-74-6

I. Title.

PS8587.M57T73 1990   C811'.54   C90-093967-2
PR9199.3.S55T73 1990

Contents

II. Toronto 1896 – 1973

III. Toronto 1987 – 1988

IV. Paris 1988

For Laureen

the flat plane deepens
forms icons in the mind's charged cells
memory invents
truth
writes it
with rivers
of light

I

Paris 1925 – 1963

"... the camera makes everyone a tourist in other people's reality, and eventually in one's own."

Susan Sontag

"J'écris avec la lumière."

André Kertész

Rue Vavin. 1925

shutters
open white
at every window
stutter of lines a
maze right-angles repeat
frame by frame

one woman stretches out
straining
to see what there is beyond
this repetition

there is no view
there is a door she has failed to open
somewhere inside

she is hung forever
in the wrong place
on a building's beaten face
where no one seeks
to see beyond the glass
beyond the shuttered pane

she calls out
her words shudder against the wall
their echo
her only answer

Zadkine in his Studio. 1926

his head at slight angle
links
muse
& music

in still light
he listens
for the movement

it pulses through him
pulls his posed
relaxed body
into rhythm

his head rocks back & forth

air sings, sighs, whines,
in the narrow gap
between his chest, eyes
wood & bronze

his hands dance
shaping
pitch & particle

Les Halles in the Early Morning. 1927

a city is a reservoir
of language
a breeding ground for words that grow
that loiter everywhere

words direct
words watch
& walk
words laugh
& entertain
words promise
words sell

with words this city
shouts commands
writes itself in
& out of control

A Butcher at Les Halles. 1927

hands on hips
six blades
slipped with a whisper
into his leather holster
& a skewer, dangling from his belt
a lean & lethal tool

he is surgeon-precise with a blade
the incision gives quick death

he wears rubber boots
stands
to his ankles
in blood & entrails

at the end of the day
he scrapes away the smell

at night
he runs his fingers
along the undulations
of neck
chest
ribs
stomach
      of a lover

    giving

& taking

with deft hands

The Famous Model Kiki. 1927

model:
plan, or prototype for removing flaws
or *epitome:*
the perfect presentation

a round face
large nose
shaded winged lips
eyebrows pencilled
blunt-cut hair dark & shiny
body broad & fleshy
crossed by her polite, folded hands
a fur coat drapes
from her shoulders
on the left collar
     hangs
a corsage of limp roses

two visions rise behind her
one of women on hands & knees
washing garments
the other of escape by sea
on wind & canvas sail

she cannot
bend or soar
with either dream

she is
painted & adorned
all made up

A Bistro. 1927

his right eye squints
closed by a scar above the brow
his left leg
a wooden peg that sticks straight out

stories written with his body
he tells for tumblers of whiskey
in bistros
to listeners who lean hard on elbows
on wooden table tops
who shift to follow voyages
of memory
who laugh with him or rage
rock back on chairs
or hush
draw close to his rasping whisper

they burn their throats with fifths
to taste his life
their own, vague phantoms
felt like the leg of flesh & bone
he still senses
moving below his left knee

A Bicycle. 1928

bicycle
abandoned
in decline
braked on the seventh step down
braces against cinder wall
front wheel turned in
ninety degrees away from motion

on the gritty wall
pitted shadows trace residues
of human travellers
transient
slipping
through time's flicker

grasp the grips tight
between palm & fingers
straighten out the wheel
slip on
bang
    down
       these
          steps
with all parts moving
glide into the light
hang on &
shout

Near the Hôtel de Ville. 1928

hands toughen on unyielding metal
machine & man
push & pull

underfoot hot coals
burn through
leather boots
on grey men who dance through steam
roll black lava
flat
into a road

in this hell
there is no elegance
no perfect roundness
no grace

soon
shapes identified by name & number
will whir & stream
these fluid veins
carry currency & dreams
strong hands will navigate
the fixed path's deceit
pursue the transient shadow
the disappearing light

Place de la Concorde on a Rainy Day. 1928

suits, portfolios
earnest gestures, hats
suggest a serious intention

men
two by two
cross glistening cobblestones
walk away
each anchored to his past
by shadows
they push against
particles that hold

still

they deal
move towards the unnegotiable
enchanted
(do they know?)
by the light

Medici Fountain. 1928

their arched repose, lingering
elevated

> his stiff body, pushing
> at the base

rustle of hair
a hand moves through

> wet leaves swish
> beneath his broom

their sensuous laughter

> his purposeful shuffle

their eyes gaze
filled
with only the other's face

> head angled down
> in concentration
> sees only his work

poses caught

stone?   flesh?

the sweeper
the swept

A Window on the Quai Voltaire. 1928

inside a carved frame
a cross separates
four panes
empty, or inhabited

space
holds them, fixed
silent, in the lower quarters

her young face, pale
passionless

his, bearded
carries age

her bare
shoulder
uncovered
breast

his chest
barely seen

their eyes dazed
emptied by distance
& what is not known

he, she, held
together
in persistent gaze
the wooden avoidance of touch

Saltimbanques at the Fête Foraine. 1929

you lean against his chest

your feet in the air

hand-standing

his back arches to hold your weight

he is your platform
you are his acrobat
you show your skills
your precarious act

faces circle you
watch, see that if you shifted slightly
he'd break in two
that you both have power & control
& hold against the strongest forces

after gasping at your impossible balances
& feeling danger &
your strength
some come forward
to the upturned hat

timid hands
toss small change

At the Group Show. 1929

giacometti
standing
staring straight out
fingering the texture of his fedora, held
in his left hand
at waist height

in the same moment
brancusi
moving his hard stone sculpture
blurs, softened by the movement
his left hand on the heavy stone
also holds his hat

giacometti's sculpted face
brancusi & his shapen stone
still
their polite hands
feeling the weight

feeling the motion

moving

still
moving

Chairs. Champs Elysées. 1929

shadows thread across
flat stone

curve of iron
delicate

a question
posed

shaded answers
re-invent the truth

fore-leg of a leaping deer
rippling school of fish
arch of her back turning
flash of tossed coins

time is light
moving

The Seine from Lady Mendl's Apartment. 1929

four slight shapes hold
slivers of light in their hands
their almost invisible lines
fishing the river's bank

no one stands on a balcony
hovering
above the seine

there should be
two lovers
gazing always
upon this *river of dreams*

paris bridges oceans
freed from fixed geography
resonates in senses, resides
in memory streams of those
who've never passed along its banks

silver river
separates hard edges, or traces
curves of encounters
sensual river
blood river that joins
ink river that edges each
person to its margins
to write a history
line upon line
drawn to the river's depth

After School in the Tuileries. 1930

each is held to his chair's light metallic line

as numbers on a clock
as alone
as suspended among trees
as shadow proves the sun
as separate
as posture has meaning
as listening
as grass underfoot tickles
as their eyes never meet
as no other place
as refusal
as reunited
as a gesture by someone else
as asleep
as a solar system, seven planets orbiting one sun
as caught
as implements that process time
as men without women
as remembering
as flesh

Rue de Vaugirard. 1931

                                    perched
                                       on
                                      edge
reminding of
the reach from earth
to heaven

a dream
seen everywhere
pretends to dream utopia

the power to soar is
anchored by the thinnest wire

Rue des Ursins. 1931

through a dark doorway
two men stand among rhymes
& do not recognize poetry
they drink inside its signs
are fixtures in its grit
& grain
inside chiselled brick & stucco

she crosses the street
never reaching the sidewalk
a staccato fissure
between the company of men
& a woman's solitude
she does not cause a man to face the light

inside the dim bar men sip
& stories grow with intoxication
sin becomes conversation &
glories well-imagined
hallucinated lines whose movement
dissipates these confines

in time
they stagger out
sunblind

    a dog is leashed
    a cat is free to drink
    the guttered water

Pont Neuf on a Rainy Morning. 1931

(skin lifting
as i graze my tongue across her belly)

wet membrane
slicks curves of cobble-stones

wind-strokes ripple river's pellicle

he strides
in topcoat & fedora
dark against the sheening sidewalk
locked mid-step
between departing & arriving

something moves
a woman & a young girl
half gone
hurry at the edge
of his world

(i cannot coax her back
despite my longing)

behind, four human
shapes slip
in shade along
the further balustrade, ghostly
after-images
without names

(i ache to hold her tightly
in the growing
& the fading
light)

A Dinner at the Café du Dôme. 1935

language swirls over heads
clusters at small tables
speaks word for word
with vigour
cuts through thick cigarette smoke
settles among plates, glasses of wine,
chunks of pungent cheese
& soft bread in crisp crusts

no one looks at anyone
in this moment
– a trick –
of angle, & shutter's flick
of their forgetting, under pressure
the preciousness
of lips, eyes, hands

the loud unspoken haunts them as
they shout
& mumble
slur & whisper
stumble against the end
of conversation

A Café. Luxembourg Garden. 1963

chill of fall
signals the folding
& stacking of chairs

straw broom rests against the stack

three women sit
talking
café talk
young
talking as if
no one can hear
sipping café-crème
between their words

a man
a lone
separated
by the angle of chairs
sits
filling the moment's gnaw
with the gesture
of a distant other

in this garden café
each one shares an edge
balanced
tipping up coffee
talking or not
stirred

soon swept

clean
out of the light

Pont Marie at Night. 1963

dusk
light mist
vague contours of persons
preoccupied, tiny
moving by, breathing in
the river's musk

stones say
permanence
in shapes
side by side
each pushing toward
the perfect arch
thrusting
against gravity
the weight of time

name them
these people / this walk
their constancy
beneath the bridge
beside the river
claim them
from light that writes a history
that brings back what is not
what insists
seen
heard
here
but no longer here

tell what these people thought
what matters

show a face
that does not
disappear

Under Pont Neuf. 1963

city's liquid throat
sings through
faces

the litany
a stone laid on tongue
after tongue

incantation draws each one
to mouth the melody
lips
continue shaping words
around a full mouth
emptying
of sound

throats narrow
choke
fall mute
brittle in tight necks

The Tree. 1963

in a slim city grove
the tremble of trees falling
still echoes

trimmed limbs lie
at river's edge

six small men
on this wedge of beach
dissect &
burn the surgeon's waste
they are charged with neatness

behind them
other men have imitated nature
sewn metal threads
shaped a silken lattice in the air
a span so
delicately poised
above this water

eyes cannot avoid
these huge bones
cracked open at the knuckles
concentric rings exposed
the layering arrested

no longer reaching up to light
dark limbs
finally
as all that breathes
fallen
lying
broken in the soil
beside the flow

The Tuileries in the Afternoon. 1963

another music clarifies
through branches
descends a cathedral
of trees, settles
on close shoulders
bare arms
lovers on benches
strain to hear
press lips & tongues
against the rasping thirst

drink at the fountain
behold the melody
let in what holds you
& whom you hold
hold on
be held

perfect pitch
sustained
intoxicates

II

Toronto 1896 – 1973

"... light, though impalpable, is here a carnal
medium, a skin I share with anyone
who has been photographed."

Roland Barthes

X-Ray Patient. Hospital for Sick Children. 1896

in a dim room
a boy sits on a high stool
feet on a box

behind him stands the doctor
hand on the switch of a new machine
a wonder that erases flesh, reveals
shadows
of bones

ray boxes are soon everywhere —
in shoe stores & hospitals
to check the fit
of skeletons

experts will find the rays rip cells
will flick off shoe store dreams
slip the boxes back
behind barriers
of lead

& this boy's bones
are they fit?
in the flicker
will his shadow dance
or shatter?

Yonge & King Streets. 1904

pulses surge
through wires that forest overhead
on rails of steel
over roads' red bricks
a spoke-wheeled snappy black tin lizzie
turns a corner
passes a horse-drawn carriage

through clang & clutter
people hustle
on cement paths
on adrenaline
past shops with canopies
beside glazed reflections
men & women sweat the metallic city
feel coin in the palm
the weight of product
on stiff shoulders

they are urged
to reach for more
are prodded to be tourists
to escape
at bargain rates

while tumbling on the wheel of light
racing time's erasure

Kids in the Ward. 1908

his jacket snug, rumpled
breeches tight at his knees

her small body lost
in a wool vest & heavy skirt

both wear scuffed boots

he, eleven years old
holds
with two hands
an umbrella
over their heads
its torn fabric
wedging open
the sky

his head is cocked
grin wide
his stance a jest
a gesture gained on streets
on broken surfaces

she, by eight years
has earned a serious brow
determined, she questions horizons
worries answers

her right hand clutches a blanket
to her chest, a vow against
cold surprise

they are not fashionable
in the robes of the ward
but fashioned

Suits Pressed. The Ward. 1909

head against hard board
body prone on wooden crate
he naps

suits pressed while you wait
15 minutes

no one wakes him
to be without a dress or suit
absurd in underwear
in a cubicle
for even a few minutes
alone with the mirror

he presses
further from the crease of vanity
deeper
into smooth sleep

Level Crossing. Sunnyside. 1910

fire blazing in the belly
belching smoke   sneezing steam
the horse churns
past the drop gate at Sunnyside
to ride steel veins
to land's extremities
to waiting hands

two men
    silhouettes cast
    on snow & steam-blast
insist the mystery of trains
lean on the gate
watch arrivals & departures

the iron horse enthralls them
hauls present into past
images to words
memory's freight
burning to the line's end

Press Photographers. Queen's Park. 1911

eight stand in line
box-cameras in hands
or on tripods
one crouches, camera on knee
head at the eye piece
lens on you
the tenth photographer, invisible

they are image morticians
for *Fox News,* the *Telegram,*
men who preserve moments
who change what's seen
who shape thought
provide charged instants
that insist we were alive

on the legislature's limestone steps
on chemical plates in tiny darkened chambers
they control the light
they catch today's story
in two dimensions
reduce and amplify at once

are caught themselves
boxed in light

Frozen Lakefront. 1911

beyond scrawny trees
sky presses water's solid skin

two figures stand
separate
shapes that duplicate
in cities whose limbs & muscles sprawl
on blemished rock & water

records are kept
in silver halide
in oil on canvas
in ink on paper
in electrons in silicon & acetate

gestures of chemistry & physics
etch our presence
bone & steel crawling over ice
into earth's layered memory

Macedonian Rooming House. King Street East. 1912

nineteen men sit or stand
with hats
in hand   or worn
above dark hair
above faces   mostly not smiling
in a narrow slot of a room
with patterned walls
& tattered carpet

here on foreign ground
in familiar dialect
they talk of jobs done   or not found

outside this room
they stumble
tongues & ears groping
tumbling over strange syllables, while
washing dishes at the Royal York
digging dank clay beneath the city at Garrison Creek
hefting stones above the streets on the Canada Life

they wear odd hats
laced boots
thick moustaches
heavy jaws.
what are their proper names?
do they hear *greek boy, greasy, dp*?
or are they shown respect
for skill & dedication?

set apart
they are far
from families & lovers kept
in mind
in small photographs
fingered in pockets

in this windowless room
they imagine windows

Sewer Construction. Garrison Creek. 1912

men dig a passage in a city's gut
young moles
tough enough to bear enclosure
far from sunlight
far from acclaim
weight of the whole earth squeezing in
arching walls & sagging timbers
threatening to draw muck down
fill nostrils & mouths
choke off damp air

close, they know
the location of each blister & scraped knuckle
the distinctive smells that hug each body
& each one's rhythm of breath

thrusting into clay
digging one another
with coarse & constant jokes
they muscle & jab
toughen
deny fear

at the end of each day
they surface
poke cautious heads out of earth
sniff dry air
squint in the glare

push up & out
tunnel
awkward, flinching
through unbounded space

Freak Show. Exhibition Midway. 1912

step right up!
for a single dime
you'll see the strangest sights!
the world's smallest mother
the fattest man ever born
cleopatra & her snakes
the dog-faced boy
the woman with alligator skin
the man who eats glass
step right up!
step right up!

for a price
behind a canvas facade
painted with exotic images
we can see the aberrations
that occur by birth
or circumstance, or fabrication
the flabby man imprisoned in his own flesh
the dwarf and her baby
the sad ugly boy

being curious
or arrogant
we laugh & point
confident, being normal

in time no tent can hold the freaks
they take the streets
their banners fly
on tv screens
in newsprint headlines

step right up!
& you will see
the hungriest girl-child
the junky
the mustard-gassed soldier
the millionaire murderer
the legless whore
& the two-faced politician
step right up!
step right up!

no charge at the door
pay on your way out!

Tub Bath. Hospital for Sick Children. 1915

edge
    of the porcelain tub
he leans on
with his left hand, for balance
                            feels
under his tentative fingers
                      cold

his arms shake
pale back bends
young buttocks goose-bump

he leans forward
from the waist
nervous
holds his thighs together
above crossed feet

the nurse's hand roughs
a cloth of cool water
on his shoulder's skin
she is capped
efficient   in a long gown

there is no comfort
in this high white corner
for his nakedness
no curing heat
to straighten his small frame

Civic Abattoir. 1914

two men
in hats   ties   topcoats
stand in the clean room
among racks of beef

behind this neat scene
the killing beds fill
with terror-bulged cows' eyes
with blood & bedlam
with flailing limbs cracking against chests
raw cries chafing ears, deafened
to any music

or silence

breathe death

see what lurks
behind hygiene
behind words like
approved,   official
know what came before public relations
hunger to stand
close to meat
on soil
in imagination's power
with knowledge moving
from bones to flesh to sky
horizon   skin   marrow

World War I Tank at City Hall. 1915

an armoured tank prowls the city square
firing rounds
blowing familiar buildings to the ground
& human bodies   part or whole   into pungent air
imagine its weight crushing you

imagine the same tank in your city square
cannon silent
skulls not shattered
but squeezed under stylish hats
faces gathered to cheer
steel, hard & thick
against skin, safe
before going home

gentle hands hold
bouncing children on knees
kind voices tell of wondrous war machines
stronger than hands & hearts
to initiate the young
to fantasies of power

imagine

death more frequent than food
children's dreams
force fed

Forging Core of 75mm Shells. Allis-Chalmers Co. 19:

silent

as the moment before prayer

three men
among vapours
before this huge forge
stand, to witness a change of state
safe, at a distance
from molten metal

elegant machines
the perfect union of commerce & science
this war

what is the price
of a 75 millimetre shell?
how many jobs will it provide?
how many people can it kill?
what is the cost per casualty unit?
what does the bar graph predict?
give me the bottom line

there is beauty
in mathematics

precision

distance

Housing. 1919

after a day
of hunting for a job
another failed day
he sits
on a low cabinet
on the sidewalk
among his furniture
cast out of warm rooms

his furniture for sale
he is thin
hungry
for a customer
    a break
    a stroke of luck

with no address
he's freed
of structure
of shelter
homeless, he's a city's discard
trapped
chained to assets
doing time
for dreaming

Arts & Letters Club. 1921

faces pattern perimeters of tables
faces with names
names imaging their way
into the future
into history
Fairley   Harris
Lismer   MacDonald
Jackson   Varley   Johnston

faces different
or the same as skin
pocked   or smooth
sombre, smiling
self-concerned or radiant

smoke moves in the back of a throat
   beer bubbles on a tongue
  a joke
              a disagreement
   worries about money
                an arthritic hand
   jealousy clawing friendship
      the musty smell of the room
the painting made that afternoon

still in them:
bristles soaking colour
soft scratch on canvas
wrist bending, straightening
to shape, shade, texture
motion leaves
signatures,
names dense with narrative
paint un-naming

Sunnyside. 1922

the midway is anxious
crowds body to body
induces vertigo.
adrenaline fires appetites
the tongue demands.
young friends jostle and laugh
introduce the boy & girl.
(in the photograph
she is pretty & demure
he is lean, handsome)

they board the roller-coaster, first car
strap in
coast
          drop
                    down
& up
        round &
   round
toss left to right
          right to
left
       dizzy
& plunge

at night they are startled
by all they do not know of skin

later there are only photographs
to probe
faces
seek a feeling, a word
an explanation
search for intention
what they saw when they fell
into each other's hearts
caromed the heady
drop
      that spun them
                  reeling
                         apart

Street Sweeper. 1923

brush strokes repeat
the sweeper sweeps the street
while model Ts bear down
no lovers in marble
to lift his eyes
no rustle of hand in hair
nothing heard over engines' cough & clatter
but the whisk,
whisk

he bends
beneath peaked cap
inside rumpled trousers
thick-soled boots
shirt with sleeves
& vest

eyes focus at his feet
where the broom   in his right hand
meets pavement
where the lip of his bag devours

his slight body turns
dances an eccentric choreography
hunks of rubber / metal / glass / paper
determine him

Western Gap Marker Buoys. 1926

fat marine carcasses
beached &
lying on their sides
are alien on land
as we are among their bulk

steel body belly-split
fleshy body ripped by scavengers

bell stations
in the sea of reverence
call the witnesses
to sacrifice

Last Stone. Canada Life Building. 1930

hung on chain
on cable
on will & fingertips
reaching for / resisting
stable state
man & stone
grapple
with gravity
with intention

high on this stony ledge
on this mountain of a building
within a measure of
their lives (deaths)
capped men
face stones' hard surface
understand balance & angles
faceless heroes who hang on
for a buck
who grunt &
nudge a large swung stone into position
force it into towering shapes
into supple compliance

in afternoon light
the final stone gleams
last cell placed in a building's skin
a skin whose every undulation
these men have touched   urged   gazed upon
known better than any wife or lover

Bren Gun Girl. 1941

          she is
assembling a weapon
          stroking smooth metal
she is independent
          alone
she thinks of soldiers
          left hand on the gun barrel

a cigarette in her right hand
smoke drifts beside her face
past bandana-held hair
          she is
in the factory / standing
          behind the boys at war

          she is flesh & blood
she is quality control
          she is an image
industrial &
          sultry
          a prop optioned
          for propaganda

she is code that speaks
more than intended
code dispatched
to foreshadow
the other breaking war

Newspaper Vendor. Yonge & Richmond. 1973

buildings peak
like bar charts
above an intersection

salaries pass
in suits
in bright ties & shined shoes

a vendor shouts
deals currency
for current information
words for appetites
words that brew
a stew of headline news
a one-stop meal of
daily bites whose
repetition gnaws to bone

words stain
push into his hand
the thin comfort
of coin
grid the corners of his eyes
gride a graph
into his brow

III

Toronto 1987 – 88

"that is a made place, created by light
wherefrom the shadows that are forms fall.

Wherefrom fall all architectures I am"

Robert Duncan

X-Ray Unit. Hospital For Sick Children. 1988

a child huddles
in a lap
in a narrow lair, surrounded

the gleaming steel moves
circles
around him
drone tightens a knot at the temple
glass eyes stare
reposition
probe him
– his rising / falling chest
   his stuttering heart –
peer toward the mystery of
the muscle that drives
its flutter
scanned, revealed on the screen
a butterfly in soft greys
out of place
on tv
in a morning cartoon

Yonge & King Streets. 1988

prestissimo

rattleclanksquealhonkconcretetoconcrete
echoesbouncingbludgeonairatmadcornerchic
cornercornerofsilks&rougeofrazorcreases
bloomage&plumagecornerbarelegsbleachedhair
belts&lacecornerofleatherbondagecorner&stocks
discussedbyassistantmanagerswhomacho-strut
cornertoself-importantcornerwomantriminwhitea
madonnastilletto-highwalkmaningplacidwith
earphone-thinhalocyclistssatsanity'sedgepeddle
onslendertube&wireamongmotorizedwarriorsin
hurlingmetalhulkssheetsteelthunderovertracks
cymbalcrashofnewestjazzcrazycacophonousurban
croonsharp-edgedcornercutslikedullaxepounds
instinctintofearintodeadlinehustlepummels
serenitytoextinctiontosirens'insistentwailas
rumblingmotorbikesgrowlroundthecorner
percolatethestreetforcharityrideforsight
amongthesighted-blind

Children. The Ward. 1988

at seventeen her
full reddened lips
hair kinked & tinted
to shoulder-blades
striped jersey tucked
at trim waist
into white shorts
above slender legs

his bright teeth
flash a man-boy smile
beneath peak-cap
above faded sweatshirt
sky-blue shorts
scuffed sneakers
awkward limbs

they spy the looking glass
from corners of eyes
vie for self-attention
their glazed shapes
fluid in reflected space
face checked against ideal face
in the silent glass

illusion whispers across the gap
she moves toward the sheen
he leans toward the silvered eye

they know too well the mirror's plane
so little of horizons

Spirit Cleaners. Yonge & Dundas. The Ward. 1988

you would cleanse
(beneath gleaming towers)
save me
(in this cathedral
of commerce)
belief   you say   is easy

gulls, toothless
scavenge at my feet
poke pizza crusts
swallow pieces whole

in heaven
dirigibles proclaim new gods
fuji   good-year   foster's

yes the agitation's thick

products do
not bring me
to my knees, though i am clipped
by this economy
its gulls that bill & beak my meal

save me?
you will not save me. no sale.
no salvation.
i am not shopping

Level Crossing. Sunnyside. 1988

on his terrace he smokes
sips from cans of Coke, watches
commuters zoom below to mimico
or oakville or to toronto's heart

thin carpet & stuffed chair
poke from his hillside cave
pop-can spout rings circle his camp
grind into earth glinty tin measures
of moments, a currency
for future archaeologists

his afternoon walk takes him
to the street
to lids he flips
reaching elbow-deep
into the muck of cast-off lunches
& laments, residues of insatiable hungers

two workmen weld metal bars
to lock him out
unofficial housing is prohibited
dwellings must be built by contractors
owned by developers
inspected by civil servants

no bars no sealed shell can block him
he sits at sight's periphery
at night's perilous edge
he sits still
outside the barred door
passed by motorists who exhilarate
at the controls
believing they choose their destinations

Press Photographer. Queens' Park. 1987

inside pink limestone skin
beyond the high foyer
across red carpet
beneath oak beams & chandeliers
government is governing

we watch from the gallery

leaders wrangle, gaze through
forests of lenses & microphones
along boulevards
toward the lake
as if with vision

we are secure

later, on television
reporters are reporting
light & sound are broken down
digitized
reassembled
into easy shapes
transmitted
shape a nation
by *coverage*
of *policy & management*

fact & lie tangle
into instant history
a dime-store bangle
that infects
beginning at the wrist

Lakefront. 1988

out of the grey haze

the cleansing rain

the acid wash

on lakes &

denims

temporary fashions of attention

fascinations

fascisms

schisms

schizophrenias of dailiness

we are in danger

the dreary & the dread engulf

we dump

to forget

amnesia drives

under this tree

there is no dry circle

only this dire space I huddle in

small

shrinking

King Street East. Macedonian Rooming House. 1988

sun blasts here
the way it might have
& might still do
& does in dreams of the mediterranean
on white-washed walls
this same sun
this changing sun

pretend a photograph has substance
that light is permanent
that clean red brick
will radiate some truth
that a cornice gargoyle
guards memory

photos tease
offer what is gone
a having / losing that confuses

wishing not to fill with emptiness
turn the photo's face away
search the thinning edge
for the dream's distraction

this street reveals no memory of light

Sewer. Stephen Drive. 1984 / 1988

i think about alligators
rats & other life
as the workman slips his pick
into the steel sewer grate

i lower my body into
        the dank gap
rubber boots plonking
on iron rungs
cool damp rising to meet me
from the gurgle of water
                rushing below

i stand ankle deep
in an antechamber
at a bend where
black slop flows
angles sharply right & roars by
into the dark

occasional waves leap the barrier
slosh into this overflow
lap grey-brown at my boots
nudge me with fecal lumps floating
among condom rings

i worry about bacteria
about storm surges
about slipping & falling
about how to climb without
touching the ladder
with bare hands

i splosh toward escape
carefully wrap my hands around
the shafts & pull myself up
toward the man hole moon
pull up out of this gut
fear nipping at my ass

Exhibition Midway. 1988

the photograph intrudes
a double that
pretends.
an old skin
shed

my face is younger
on my mother's wall

shouts of the crowd echo

behind the stadium
freaks grin in tents for pocket change
athletes & rock stars
don spectacular identities

i sit in bleachers
the spotlight bleeds a semblance
of divine illumination
i devour images
live in fear's dark
& lies to keep the fear at bay
cheer madly
for the light outside me
its distant skin

Hospital Ward. 1967 / 1988

waking from anaesthetized sleep
feeling dizzy &
tender in the abdomen
in the deep cut
he reaches into the dark

he touches nothing
no one
not even the old man, wheezing
in the bed across the room

he sinks back
drifts in a dream:
he is sleeping in the bed across the room

in a day he can sit up

& in another, walk

with his first steps
he crosses the cold floor
touches the pale hand

next day
his companion is his passenger
in a wheel chair
they steer through long hallways
wheel through corners
through the maze
spin fluorescent circles
reel in the antiseptic gleam
as one.

they break
the barrier of unsound
                              bodies
refuse to turn in pain's dark spiral

Abattoir Findings. 1988

1.

A proper stick means a fast bleed
& a quick blackout for the hog.
If the hog is suspended,
steady it by placing the flat of the hand
on the shoulder (do not grasp the leg)
& insert the knife
several inches in front of the breast
with the point of the knife directed
toward the tail
give an upward thrust
dip the point until it strikes the backbone
then withdraw it.

2.

Slit the hind leg tendons
then hoist the cow into the air
on the tractor lift.
Let the blood drain
then split the belly.
The organs will slide out.
They will be startling shades
of green & purple. This is normal.
(Throw these to the dogs.)
Skin & portion the meat.

3.

A dull knife is inefficient
& ineffective except for cutting oneself.
Those of us who marvel
at the skill & dexterity of the men
working in the slaughter rooms
of large & small packing houses
must remember that these men
work with sharp tools
& must be expert to hold their jobs.

4.

"At the counter
we do not encourage
the connection
between the living animal
& that lovely wrapped steak."

City Hall Square. 1987

exuberant in brisk air
children glide or stumble on ice
with or against
a west wind
that stings

old & new architectures
bracket a history
that ghosts this town square
where war has been glorified
its dead mourned
remembered with monuments
& a symbol for peace
in grey stone, weathered wood
with water & flame
& clinging shrubs
where sparrows skitter
among leaf & rock
peck seeds & insects
sip from dropped berries

a vine sends roots deep into pores
clutches, undermines
rock, breaks it down
to stone
to dust scattering on the wind
amidst innocent laughter

Allis-Chalmers Co. 1988

think of that which eludes thought
concentrate
spindle the thinking outward
let it thin like topsoil in winds
that march over parched prairie

thought can be like this
or can be this
or perhaps not

thought alone cannot destroy

thought by itself cannot build
boundaries, bombs
or a lone tractor
sitting empty in a fenced field

a factory cannot be located
though it has spun
web-like over contintents
permitted bankruptcy in ailing branches

thought can retell the story

they say
amputation allows what remains
to strengthen

think the thought
of the dead limb

Housing / Streets. 1988

a man shuffles
along the sidewalk on bathurst street
wears layers of grime
beneath a knotted beard
clutches stuffed white plastic bags
in stained fists
his feet shuffle
shuffle, shoeless
on the hot concrete

she is mound-shaped, bulging
like the bags she pushes
in carts, squeaking along bloor street
from alcove to alley
from a dark grubby face
her cracked & toothless mouth crumbles
mumbles shadows
of words

lying on his right side
on a slim aluminum bed
in the glass waiting-booth
on spadina avenue
the acrid man snores
his left pant-leg hangs limp.
    outside the glass wall
    that shelters him
    in the gutter
    lies
    his man-made limb

in my house i wonder
which chair becomes my throne
which table feeds my longing
which toy stills my greed
which cabinet houses my rage
which drawer contains my desire
which furniture can free me?

Modern Clubs. 1988

behind the smooth mask
the face is gnarled
greed's grin intransigent

beneath the surgeon's blade   skin
lifts
liposuction stills insecurity
feeds sutured vanity

schoolboys lock
& roll in rage
on the yard's rough floor
young girls grimace
clench at clumps of hair

screams knife the air

the clawing ache gnaws flesh raw
bandages of fine gauze suffocate the wound

stakes grow
the prize diminishes

an eye sights down a rifle barrel

a foot crushes a cocoon

hands caress a gold bar

machines surround the forest

fingers close around a throat

the sweat
too many bodies
too bare
too close

the reaching towards
of untouching hands

Sunnyside. 1988

tossed coins clink on plates
on test-your-strength, a whack & gong
the crack of guns & bullseye-pings
on the shooting range
& the chorus of the barker's call
fool me with your weight
win a kewpie doll

the casual brush of bodies
the clasp of hands
the light of a gone lover, aroused

there is
no game of chance
no scent of french fries
no thrill ride
no cotton candy
no heart spin to follow eyes

lips to blazing tar
kiss this long wide stretch of pavement
bliss is driven far
                    far off

Street Sweeper. 1988

two orange men flare
in mercury vapour night
in ritual dance.
they circle festering clumps
grasp with gloved hands

they feed the growling machine
that gobbles plastic
gulps noxious liquids that seep
from sopping cardboard
snorts any food into its belly
digests it into dense turds

the phosphorescent men
grab the handle
heave up
clutch the lurching truck
pivot toward the reeking bin
grimy carriage footmen riding
to the smouldering nuisance ground

Western Gap. 1988

sugar brew
as sweet as chewing gum
bubbles from malting stacks
melts into morning

passion is loose in two who touch
at the end of a long bench
at the end of a night of longing & desire
good-byes promise the ache
the delicious ache

a sleek beach
rises
perpendicular at lake's edge
reaching for
& pushing out
the dreamy sky

dark clouds thunder
predators chase deals
all is malled & plundered
carcasses scatter round the nest
eyes gulp strangers
the membrane grows
thin beneath the mask

ah! the malt-sweet air

Canada Life Building. 1988

fifteen stories below the beacon
i imagine the height
the stomach's quiver
the dizzy dance of vertigo

grounded
i sit in grid-lock
crawl of bodies cased in costly shells
(cocooned larvae seeking wings)

in a blue & tufted sky
sun settles on the building's highest corner
a blade of shadow penetrates
slicing light
   (parceled out
   taken by degrees)
from us who creep beneath

i try to comprehend the height's seduction
the unthought throw of body into space
the free
      fall
how we plunge
& then negotiate
with gravity
what awkward flappings our arms make
the flurry that feigns flight

Factory. Strachan Avenue. 1988

foreigners are no longer enemies
offering grenade souffle
& mustard-slick bayonets
but friends
who drive the lunch wagon
or sit next to you with a sandwich
outside the factory

    a cadet in khaki uniform cycles by
    toward the armoury
    for her day parade

    (1941:
    the bren gun girl
    walks slowly from the trolley-stop
    toward the same factory
    – the weapons factory –
    crossing train tracks
    in dim lamplight
    cloaked in the weight of war)

today flags flutter above the gate.
the production line churns out appliances.
the company flag flies
beside the flag of canada, signals alliance
of country & commerce, a wealth built
over graves.
the corporate headstone gleams in neon.
the slogan signboard flashes:
                                           never
                                      never do
                                  never do a
                            never do a wrong
                      never do a wrong to
                never do a wrong to make
            never do a wrong to make a
        never do a wrong to make a friend
      never do a wrong to make a friend or
    never do a wrong to make a friend or keep
  never do a wrong to make a friend or keep one

Newspaper Vendor. Bay & King. 1987

whipping wind
rips ties
from jackets
ruffles permanents
into askew haloes
that frame
cosmeticized faces
close-shaved skin-braced faces
beneath a cloud-blown heaven
glimpsed on glass
vast & vertical

beside the flow of   autos   buses   trolley cars
& people on bicycle & foot
two stand out
not moving with the pace
not hustling dollar signs
but drifting in slow motion
the currency of love, delirium
in their eyes

through cables underground
or in beams to satellites
electrons transfer dollars & commodities
on the international exchange

on the corner
metal bangs under a fist
coins jangle
hands rattle the jammed door
a boot slams against the steel
the box holds
refuses to release

IV

Paris. 1988

"La fenêtre s'ouvre comme une orange
Le beau fruit de la lumière"

Guillaume Apollinaire

Rue Vavin. 1988

quilting
at this window
her slow hands
her quilting hands
her lining face
her whitening hair

the blanket of years pattern her
beside potted chrysanthemum
redder on her balcony

what lies behind shutters that bracket her
shutters she closes
that close her in

i imagine her wrinkled hands
steady on needle & cloth
stitching her warmth
into the geometry
of a sleeper's life

on the street, vavin
va vin
we go on in the days' journey
jour née
each day
      severed from the night-dark rope
we are born
to streets we walk   ride   run
or are rueful on

vin
from the vined fruit
stitched into hillsides
we savour the wine
with or without vanity
blanc ou rouge
our cheeks warming

we slip
through twined streets
teeming with strangers
who thread their way
in the city
companions cross-stitched
beneath reddest chrysanthemums

Osip Zadkine's Studio. 1988

breath
drawn
a shaped gasp pulls
a hole
in poet's body

empty space
carved in metal & wood
into silence   & breath
into figures, a crowd
of shapes
hands on instruments or
upraised, clutching the invisible

hidden
in a courtyard on rue d'Assas where
with caliper & saw, mallet & plier
with knife & eye
his fingers cut
from nothing
from all he knew
bodies' joy   or anguish

in this garden
trees he walked among
whose leaves he touched
still grasp for sun as he did
shaping line & lustre
in black, orange, gold, mossy blue
in elm, ebony, brass, bronze,
ink on paper

grand windows
welcome the light
he loved, transformed
for his own
& later coming eyes

though he still moves here
in bodies, in songs that remain
the ivory keys of his accordion
are silent

his apron's stringy arms hang limp
no body
to embrace
his substance borne
beyond the melody of
breath

Forum des Halles. 1988

A

D

E E

F

I I

L   L

M

N

O   O

R

S

T

U   U

V

blue light
from glass screens
rains over
those who
from underground
churn up
through the chrome throat
tonguing air
& spilling
a glut of syllables

as each one pauses
or passes on
the screens puff up
shatter one image into thirty-six fragments
or repeat one image thirty-six times
pix factored by faces
who turn to watch
the new language
la langue qui danse
in the pixillated stage
les images d'un âge
of outered space

in Paris   in Zimbabwe   in North America
in the universe   in the cinema   on television
in the forum des halles   in shopping malls
everywhere   all   everyone   in image-moments
compressed   to an equation   a mathematics
that refuses answers

l'espace que la vidéophonie a transposé
à l'intérieur de chaque personne

the world's to be consumed
le monde des aliments

beneath grey clouds

    kite-sailing

                  stone-plunged
    in or out of love
        of a job
  of trouble

                          of grace
our fragments
      fall
        the sentence is
assigned
nous sommes engagés
words broken   before we speak
      rough edges will not elide

ingurgités
en passant
dans la banque de l'image

Butcher at Les Halles. 1988

the butcher has moved
to rue de Petit Carreux
jewel that glitters
lit windows overflowing
with the gleam of fresh food
brilliant greens of romaine, epinards
haricots jaunes, courgettes
reds of tomates,
purple betteraves, et chou
the pink, blue, crimson
of meats of chicken, cow, rabbit, pig
horse, deer
neck-slung duck & pheasant
plucked, chopped, sliced
or hung whole & cloaked
in fur & feather

we eat
time   devours us
centuries leave us behind
we work, talk, occasionally pray
we pay
we love
with or without passion

on rue St. Denis
doorways hug bodies
that beckon gritty trade

down the street
toward les halles
sex shops tender flesh
pink & brown meat
where skin is a rendering of lens & film
of light, tissue too thin
to touch
tactile enough to ignite
the lonely dream

thin
line
of
chin
lips
nose
eyes
ears
holding
you
together
making
of   nothing
a life-lined face
drawn through   time
that pushes features
into relief

curved pull of slim wire
slipped you through
his eyes

he's defined your mouth prim
removed rouge & shadow from you
hung your eyes in air's socket
made a pert rocket of your nose
pursued you in aluminum
replaced you
displayed you, a museum piece
now encased
not free nor fiery
as you lived

yet
over & over
you push
through
barriers
shine
along
a slender line
that draws
you outside your time
that draws
eyes
& holds them
to you

Bar aux Balcons. 1988

stuck, cornered
at butte's edge
rumpled at the bar
smooth glass in hand
brandy finding
amidst thick beard
his lips
his mouth that mumbles curses
at trucks that pass
between sips
lugging stone remains
of architecture
that once textured his days
his passage ways

if he could
his ears would block the rumble
with enough hands he'd hold up walls
drive the trucks away

he sets down his glass   empty
as gaping streets

his chair slips backwards
down the butte
out of control
toward pere lachaise
    (with graves of proust, piaf,
    stein, wilde,
    morrison & apollinaire
    where sun fell soft & orange
    on my sorrow)

he stands, grasps the door handle
ceramic, white
pure & smooth in his palm
steps toward the crumbling street
stops

tightens his grip
on the comforting sphere

Abandoned Bicycle. 1988

a bicycle leans on a steel pole
not jostling in traffic
not bearing any alfred jarry
any known or unknown rider

alfred jarry
where are you?
i need you
i am here
beneath a proscenium of sky
below this bent moon
under the pantheon dome
beside the stone wall
by the gutted shop

in the cold night
in lamp-light glow
people rush on foot
pushed by the bite
cars are jumping curbs
crushing bicycle wheels

come to the stage jarry
bring your pistol
they're shell-gaming us
they're ramming the bike against the pole
forcing a rattle in its hollow bones

speak to us jarry
fire bullets through the ceiling
through the scrim of time
through the curtain of belief

we've forgotten
the props are papier-mâché
the actors wear masks
the audience has been replaced by marionettes

    the regularity of breathing
    is so gentle
    we are hardly aware of it
    or the whisper of a cycle
    passing

Near Hôtel de Ville. 1988

a door opens

i would not have you enter
this way
as memory
stepping through
the oak door frame in '70
& rooms so many times since

i long to have you here
in your own chair
at your dark wooden table
or any other one
sharing my same light

water sprays my right cheek
i squint into sun
a metal knot of cars
grumbles & squeals in my ears
mopeds & diesels & plumes of blue exhaust
are sucked through blacktop veins.
the seine glitters
blows fresh breath
sails islands.
trees thicken
weep into the river
or flourish green
higher into sky.
fountain waters hiss & dance.
bell-chimes punctuate.

cement is cold & hard beneath me
wind chills my back
my pencil dulls
my imagination shrinks in this
turgid world i'm left
                          out in
trying to write that other shade
or flare, that shadow, gleam
we hardly see
                    or feel
moving
a longer or
shorter time
while breath graces
the hidden blossoms
of our lungs

for bpNichol

Place de la Concorde on a Cold Morning. 1988

an old woman tosses crumbs
pigeons cluster
tri-colour flags flash messages
in a granite sky

an ancient monolithic tongue moves in a mouth
of air
speaks without sound

words burst
alight in the mind
drawn
as if through lens
to flame

across the square
a lion stalks
in a flash of compositions
by photographers
walks again & again
muscles rippling the frame

a man edges
past baring trees
toward the cobbled road
bitter wind tears the eye
bites beneath the skin
street lamps glow
punctuate his clouding breath

Fontaine de Maria de Medici. 1988

repose
the posture love takes
unguarded, as stone's curve
the curves of two carved
craving & tender
under a protective god
whose angels' urns
tumble melody down temple walls
praising love's tranquility

his raised knee stays her back
arm cradling her head
her torso turned to him
her hand in his hair
their locked gaze

sparrows, pigeons, strut & bathe
attendants, spurred by seasons
replace, pot by pot, rosy impatiens
with yellow chrysanthemum
stroller, sitter
deity or priest, reader
lovers who caress
writers who scribble the tissue of
their thought
all witnesses

i ache
for those i have loved
& do love, whose absence draws me down
with the weight of my flawed promises

A Window on Quai Voltaire. 1988.

cliches are correct
everything changes
nothing changes

two heads
are framed by windows
above the street

they've aged
sixty years
have turned them
by degrees, away
to face into a room

warm light graces them
perhaps they laugh
at tricks they play with time
turning
like a river's curve
& doubling back as water does
til cycling to face, again
the view
the street i age in

inhabitants of windows
search glazed holes
for reference
for answers that transparency appears
to hold

Dancer. Centre Pompidou. 1988

lento

shifting   in air   on stone

gestures   tight   as shadow's

scarce   body

in   black   moves

not   to   be   still   wind   whispers

crinkles   thin   blue   film   fingers

hold   fingers   pinch   space

within   without

brackets   a   syllable   of   air

courts   takes   in   lets   go

almond   eyes   closed   search

within   music   whose   metallic   melody   is

mood   &   tempo   though

impossible   blue   film   begins   to

cover   inch   by   inch

gesture   replaces   empty   space   in   wind

blown   blue   replaces   wind   in   blue

melts   into   cobble   grid   tucking

blue   beneath   curled   smallest

now   blue   tight   at   edges

tight   over   down-turned

head   hands   crossed

tiny   blessed   body

rocking   rocking   rocking

Musée National d'Art Moderne. 1988

brancusi's sleeping
muse   a gleaming head
weighs.
across the room   the gold-combed rooster
breaks the barrier of sleep
rakes into morning.
out of streaked marble
grey & white
seal stretches
reaching
out of dream
into light's shape
line's grace brancusi felt
seduced by
reduced form to

struck by
giacometti's
quirky
hand
lines
thin
as pencil
or nail
pushed into
canvas
hover
between
passing
remaining
tremble
between
spaces

stretch
between
being
& not
time presses
flesh
puckers it
pocks it
it sags
from
heights
dissolves in rooms
into
thin
air

Chairs. Champs-Elysées. 1988

Avenue des Champs-Elysées Union de Banques a Paris Union de Banques a Paris
Change Change Cambio Wechsel AUDIO VIDEO FLOPPY DISKS TDK COIN-
TREAU Pakistan International PICON PICON STYLOS PARKER Librairies
BIRET SPECIALISTE DU STYLO TAX FREE SOUVENIR DE PARIS DARRA
CENTRAL INTERIM saggel vendôme BUREAU A LOUER 950 M2 DIVISIBLE
RICHARD ELLIS BURTIN BRASSERIE DE L'ETOILE 33 Record dab bier
BRASSERIE DE L'ETOILE chair chair chair chair chair chair chair RONSARD
BOUTIQUE PIERRE CARDIN cinémas GEORGE V crocodile DUNDEE II Le
monde entier l'adore Emmanuelle 6 Dirty Dancing LE NOM DE LA ROSE UN
PRINCE A NEW YORK CINEMA TOUS LES JOURS BALLY BALLY BALLY
BALLY BALLY PIZZA TUBORG BEER VESUVIO BISTRO ITALIEN
TUBORG BEER RISTORANTE GRILL PIZZA VESUVIO TUBORG BEER
VESUVIO BISTRO ITALIEN TUBORG BEER chair chair chair chair chair chair
chair chair chair chair chair chair cinemas GEORGE V STALLONE RAMBO III
L'étudiante UNE AFFAIRE DE FEMMES Le vie est un long fleuve tranquille Iraqi
airways MAISON DU DANEMARK RESTAURANT COPENHAGEN MAISON
DU DANEMARK ROYAL COPENHAGEN ROYAL COPENHAGEN
COPENHAGUE RESTAURANT FLORA DANICA RESTAURANT FIAT DEL-
EGATION COMMERCIALE D'ITALIE FIAT Alitalia McDonald's McDonald's
McDonald's McDonald's McDonald's VOLVO MPS MONTE DE PASCHI DI
SIENA BANQUE FONDEE EN 1472 PEUGEOT TALBOT 405 Flue voiture de
l'année 1988 hutchinson hutchinson BISTRO ROMAIN BISTRO ROMAIN
BURGER KING BURGER KING BURGER KING LE MENU DE LUXE A 20F
AU LIEU DE 27.70F CAFE GEORGE V BRASSERIE RESTAURANT CAFE
GEORGE V BRASSERIE chair chair chair chair chair chair chair chair chair chair
chair chair chair chair chair chair chair chair chair chair LES FOURRURES
MiLADY ACHETEZ AUJOURD'HUI AVEC 0F ET PAYEZ EN 89 LES FOUR-
RURES MiLADY DUTY FREE DETAXE A L'EXPORTATION MERCEDES-
BENZ MERCEDES-BENZ UGC NORMANDIE BIG TOM HANKS L'ART DE
LA SECURITE COGNAC CAMUS NAPOLEON NORMANDIE TOM HANKS
BIG BRUCE WILLIS PIEGE DE CRISTAL LA MAISON DE JADE ROGER
RABBIT LIDO OLYMPUS OLYMPUS PHOTO OLYMPUS PHOTO OLYMPUS
OLYMPUS OLYMPUS ENDOSCOPE OLYMPUS LUMINANCE MICRO-
SCOPE OLYMPUS AUDIO TOSHIBA VIDEO TOSHIBA COPIER JOKER
JOKER JOKER jus de fruits JOKER JOKER Audemars Piguet RIBOUREL
Heyraud Heyraud Heyraud Heyraud VERNET VERNET VERNET VERNET
VERNET VERNET QUICK ELYSEES RESTAURANT GRILL PATISSERIE
BAR CAFE QUICK ELYSEES GRILL KICKERS J.M.WESTON ROLEX AIR
AFRIQUE ROLEX CLARENCE ASSURANCES CENTRALES DE FRANCE
LEROY LEROY LEROY LEROY LEROY OPTIQUE LEROY LEROY OPTI-
CIEN THE FIRST NATIONAL BANK OF BOSTON Elysées FIRST AVENUE
PARFUMERIE PRET A PORTER CLAUDE Champagne JACQUART Reims
CHEMISE PLAY-BOY CRAVATE CHEMISE PLAY-BOY CRAVATE CHAR-
TREUSE ELNASR FRANCE TURQUIE ANDRE TURQUIE SERVICE
D'INFORMATION GODIVA CHOCOLATIER Maiffret STUDIO 102 discothèque
STUDIO 102 MONSIEUR ELYSEES MONSIEUR ELYSEES LINEA DONNA
MONSIEUR ELYSEES MONSIEUR ELYSEES MONSIEUR ELYSEES MON-
SIEUR ELYSEES MONSIEUR ELYSEES piano bar Cascades Elysees Tuborg
Cocktails LUNCH CAFE SALON DE THE chair chair chair chair chair chair chair

chair chair chair chair chair chair chair chair chair chair NATALYS NATALYS NATALYS LIGHT LIGHT LIGHT LIGHT CREDIT SUISSE MANFIELD MANFIELD Yves Rocher Yves Rocher LE TRIOMPHE DROWNING BY NUMBERS UN FILM DE PETER GREENAWAY demain c'était la guerre un filme de YOURI KARA le HASARD 9 1 / 2 SEMAINES BOUYGUES MAISON BOUYGUES point d'or LIBYAN ARAB AIRLINES OFFICE NATIONAL DE TOURISME DE THAILANDE CLUB MEDITERRANE PANCALDI FRANCE CLUB MED CLUB MED SKIEZ CLUB MED TOURISME EGYPTIEN CHARLES JOURDAN CHARLES JOURDAN THE ECONOMIST CLUB PERNOD LOWENBRAU MUNICH RESTAURANT BRASSERIE GALERIE DES CHAMPS SOHO TAKE 5 2 NIVEAUX DE BOUTIQUES NATIONAL BANK OF PAKISTAN BIMAN BANGLADESH AIRLINES TON SUR TON TON SUR TON TON SUR TON LA BRIOCHE DOREE LA BRIOCHE DOREE BREL BREL fnac fnac infinitif CABARET DES CHAMPS ELYSEES ARCADES DU LIDO 40 Boutiques dans une Galérie de Prestige Blanc Bleu Paris Blanc Bleu Paris Blanc Bleu Paris Blanc Bleu Paris F. PINET F. PINET F. PINET POINT SHOW LOISIRS CLARIDGE GALERIES du CLARIDGE PIZZAZZ STALLONE RAMBO III MIDNIGHT RUN IRONWEED MAX TISSUS MAX TISSUS Guerlain Guerlain Guerlain Lido Musique Guerlain Guerlain FERINEL GROUPE PELEGE CAFE de COLOMBIE GAUMONT CHAMPS ELYSEES Ce film est tiré du roman de NIKOS KAZANTZAKI "Le Dernier tentation" il n'est pas une adaptation des évangiles MARTIN SCORCESE LA DERNIER TENTATION DU CHRIST BRED POINT SHOW LINEA OMO LINEA OMO PROCREDIT PROCREDIT PROCREDIT PROCREDIT PROCREDIT PROCREDIT PROCREDIT PROCREDIT PROCREDIT PROCREDIT freetime freetime freetime freetime freetime freetime freetime freetime freetime PRISUNIC PRISUNIC PRISUNIC PRISUNIC VIRGIN MEGASTORE VIRGIN MEGASTORE VIRGIN MEGASTORE SEIKO SEIKO virgin virgin virgin virgin virgin virgin virgin virgin Ronyi PARFUMERIE VIRGIN MEGASTORE ON NE FERA JAMAIS ASSES DE PLACE A LA MUSIQUE LOCATEL LOCATION VIDEO GALERIE ELYSEES LA BOETIE DE VERLI DE VERLI EDMOND EDMOND STULHER STULHER Groupe Pelloux Groupe Pelloux Groupe Pelloux Groupe Pelloux Groupe Pelloux Groupe Pelloux Groupe Pelloux Groupe Pelloux KELLY SERVICES KELLY SERVICES KELLY SERVICES KELLY SERVICES KELLY SERVICES KELLY SERVICES KELLY SERVICES KELLY SERVICES Gaumont Ambassade L'OURS P.E.L.L.E LE CONQUERANT BANK TEJARAT CHANGE CHANGE Verlaine Verlaine Verlaine hamburger Quick Restaurant Quick Quick LE COLISEE LE COLISEE chair chair chair chair CITROEN HIPPO CITROEN GRILL RESTAURANT GRILL HIPPO CITROEN BAR RESTAURANT HIPPO CITROEN GRILL RESTAURANT Planar de Thomson Planar de Thomson Planar de Thomson UN ZENITH POUR LE OUI UN ZENITH POUR LE OUI UN ZENITH POUR LE OUI UN ZENITH POUR LE OUI UN ZENITH POUR LE OUI UN ZENITH POUR LE OUI UN ZENITH POUR LE OUI UN ZENITH POUR LE OUI RODIN RODIN RODIN RODIN TISSUS RODIN TISSUS RODIN RODIN MODE TISSUS LES PRIX LE MADRIGAL LE MADRIGAL chair INSTITUT PAB CITIBANK CITIBANK CITIBANK COMPAGNIE GENERALE DE BANQUE CITIBANK CHANGE ELYSEES 26 ELYSEES 26 ELYSEES 26 Galérie Elysées 26 Galérie Elysées 26 Galérie Elysées 26 Galérie Elysées 26 CAREL GALERIE ELYSEES ROND POINT PARFUMS SILVERMOON BEAUTE Avenue de Champs Elysées

The Seine near Lady Mendl's Apartment. 1988

an old fisherman is
knowledge using a long
long pole to
fish the seine

by green water
an archaeology begins
moss creeps the stone bank
a tree grows imperceptibly
pigeons poke cracks
a dog sniffs the fisher's basket

time appears to stop

but only hesitates

like his refusing fish

After School in the Tuileries. 1988

hoops roll, hoops bounce
orange   yellow   green
one blue & airborne
lodges in a beech tree

gardeners stand, bend, kneel
before a corps of statues
crop shrub & flower
from the chilling ground

a man & woman huddle, keep
the fire

a lump lies on a bench, nuzzles
a pillow of plastic-bags

ancient buildings stain
trees unleaf to skeletons
tiny dogs, just hair & bone
scatter pigeons feasting
on bugs & seeds

children climb an iron fence
thrill on the outside edge

a whistle trills.
its shrillness reigns in
circles of jibes & laughter
children surround a bench
pull on sweaters & coats
line up in twos
set off
across the park
a tingle
of shouts trailing

i walk the other way
cross dark bars low sun makes of trees
walk into the growing silence
the straightening of lines

Rue Vaugirard. 1988

love may be delicate
graceful as a bird
planing on thermals
buoyed up & up

a feather of light slivers
into the canyon-street

it is right to love before stained
facades
beneath vaulting stained glass
to breathe in night's narrow air
to whisper in the ear's cathedral
to enter the secret dark of other
to arch or coil
closer than beside
toward the petals of the rosing sun

love flies freely here
proliferates like post cards
clutters like tourists
intoxicates like
nothing described by simile

Rue des Ursins. 1988

shoulder nudges pitted wall
foot & knee brace on iron rail
in the chill, the back-bone shudders

no door remains
no words come easy
under congealing sky

facing blocks

older? newer?

does it matter?

something behind this wall
calls, a faint echo
– the clatter of glasses
  chatter of voices

a man, a woman
walk by,
not hearing
not peering at the face
mine, or the one i gaze upon
light-scarred

in the tight alley
no one's noise
or silence

old men   gone
the woman   dog & cat   all
dashed to dust

the lantern too is gone
to light what dark?

nothing known

speaking

of nothing

to the absent

Pont Neuf. Early Morning. 1988

sun slips spire to spire
its fiery tongue licks up inky sky
i risk morning's crisp edge
elbows on cement
cast early on the job
coaxing words

a greying woman on a balcony
sprinkles, from a small green can
her small box of pink flowers

the sign-changer
pastes a poster on the kiosk
Le Spectacle: Une Femme sans Histoire

from the chimney of the river barge
smoke wanders
wisps drunk up by glowing sky

gestures form life   stories
plots shape each of us
secretly
undeniably

even this movement of your eyes

Le Dôme Montparnasse. Déjeuner. 1988

perfect   smooth cuff   crisp collar   whitest shirt
black jacket   quick hands   gleam of silverware   *vous*
avez choisi monsieur? oui huîtres no.3 claire s' il vous
plait.   polished sheen of glass   brass crêpe de chine
a plate placed   neat bread   lemon bowled butter   oysters
on barnacled shells   on ice   tingle slick & cool on tongue
cork screw twist   uncorked   rose sancerre roger neveu
whispers into glass   sipped   gentle in the mouth   eye
travels grained surfaces   dark wood   supple leather
linen'd white table   white napkin   pink blossoms spray
from ceramic vases   *sole de l' île d' yeu cuite a l' huile*
d' olive aux petites légumes nouveaux   sole crossed with
slips of green onion   balanced   with thinnest carrot
potatoes round   tiny   with matched tomatoes   sole flakes
on the fork in heavier oil   i reach   the waiter's hand
fills my glass

diners   with business   or pleasure   on their minds   style
on their shoulders   women in groups   men on expense
accounts courting women   families with children   all of
means

i scratch syllables onto blue pad   pale blue against white
cloth   conversation swells toward the ceiling   beside
octagonal china   behind nouveau lettering   the Dôme
jams with words   to bursting

we are all speaking   eating from stylish plates   each
served by five attendants   i weigh the cost   the weight
these words must have   to meet the bill's preponderance   this
extravagance   my brush with reputation   to say i've
taken lunch there   myself   with ghosts of   apollinaire
modigliani   hemingway   picasso   sartre   &

my attention is drawn   i turn   glance   over my left
shoulder   samuel beckett   stares   from a frame   a
photograph   he gazes past   to outside   where
sparse leaves   shudder   on baring branches

A Café. Luxembourg Garden. 1988

passing through this garden
each one is haloed
exceptional in the palace of
an afternoon's gradient

no angels pull at my sleeve
nor beggars
a shadow breaks the page in two

wind protests
gusts until i start to write again

i am grateful.
she arrives tomorrow
to join me
to be together, gazing
upon blooms of floral light

cameras click
as if photography invents
this city
as if the camera
sanctifies our footsteps.
i stare
try to glimpse the frame   the line
sun glares
i see glint & radiance
pink & yellow petal spills
silhouettes of
torsos of trees

sparrows skitter among chair legs
leaves scuffle over gravel

green table top
plate with scattered crumbs
drained foam-traced glass
this page
my grey-gloved hand
pushing

Pont Marie at Night. 1988

I.

small human shapes
walk their own narrative
through thin amber light

definition is lost
a language we recognize
becomes uncertain

what do we articulate
beneath this darking sky by
crossing over
or under
or arching in love

a bateau floats its own daylight
dazzles the bridge
& lovers
    their black shroud ripped away
hold
& are returned
to a cocoon of dark

i too am light-blind
beneath the arc's echo
i stop
before the steep plunge
sit hard against a stark rail
feet on curved stones
my eyes play tricks
trip me up
in after-image
you
dissolved from this slight earth
appear
    a jewelled crown
    cast to the dark water

Pont Marie at Night. 1988

II.

In Memoriam bpNichol

this bridge cracks
across the river's spine
a vertebrae
lending mobility

these bones walk my thoughts to you
to your own bones grown stiff
then still
now flamed to ash

you walked in Paris in '85
perhaps this bridge
pain firing through your hip
the secret bundle of fibre
growing at your spine
clump jabbed at
by the surgeon's knife
that, trying to save
claimed you

i sit here
as if anaesthetized
feeling daily
shock & loss
though tears refuse to come

you move now
bridging distant rivers
freed of the encumbrance of your body
the way your spirit
moved in life
your eyes & words
healing many
tumorous with their own pain

i walk
with you
in the light that always burns

your light
your light

Pont Neuf. 1988

under the stone-
faced gargoyles
under the smooth arc
that frames the seine
two men design, begin to build
in view of the bridge of change
by bateaux that lure
tourists to river-edged romance

this arching chamber
echoes with furor
from above
a human river poured from hospitals
screams of a system's ills
growls *en grève*

underneath
undisturbed by protest, the labourers
construct their tiny home
of corrugated paper
& slats of wood
one wall,
then the next
to chest height.
they stretch out a third, a curtain
of accordion-fold cardboard
the fourth is ancient stone

eventually the marchers pass
& fade
traffic streams the bridge
walkers search unfolded maps for bearings
a mother spins her son in dizzy circles
tourist buses fill & roar away

vladimir & estragon stand back
admire their architecture   .
with grand
& fervent gestures

Trees. Pont des Arts. 1988

they say *it's a jungle*
monkeys slung
on vines
spiders webbed
in branches
snakes circling limbs

this tribe
   in blue with orange hats
   saws whining against
   stray or aging limbs
roars through thin forest
clumsy-footed
beside the river that beckons sun
captures its glint
in flint-shards, spinning
splintering
in a breeze-brisk flight

this is not about trees
cleared forever from the edge
though it could be
or about a river's ceaseless flow.
this is about a young woman
in black
at the end of this wall

   she is a pencil line i keep
trying to erase
from this poem
a trace that stays in sight
insisting
   she sits alone
thinking
or perhaps heart-broken,
struck by tragedy,
lost

my thoughts reach for hers
seek the thinnest link
shall we dance
with the current
                    or sink
in the undertow

neither happens
as sun flattens, egg-shaped
nests amid chimney stacks
as each evening
with
or without her
or me

tigers mewl from the leaves.
the stone wall (the trees once buffeted)
grips iron rings
embedded to hold
no tethered boats
nor the whisper of wind

The Tuileries in the Afternoon. 1988

i step into the precise
place you stood
(camera in hand) 25 years before
i feel (in) your eyes
the excitement of discovery

benches the same
curve of lion's stone back
the same
the chestnut's branches
hardly changed

a solitary man
sits, gazing down the aisle of trees
i imagine this is you
seeking another angle
bench hard against your spine

you reach into your bag for the leica
to probe the future
snap it into present
to capture one more instant

you push a comb through your grey hair
put on a black cap
you do not turn
it is forbidden
the barrier of time
impenetrable

you stand up
(i must finish now)
you move slowly toward the frame's limit
with effort
your feet scuff chestnut leaves
you edge the branching
arch, the doorway
of light & shadow
of memory

shimmering

Acknowledgements

"Western Gap. 1988" appears under another title, and "Le Dôme
Montparnasse. Déjeuner. 1988" in *The New Quarterly,* Vol. IX, No. 4,
Winter 1990.

"Rue Vavin. 1988." in *The Journal of Wild Culture,* Vol. II, No. 2 / 3, Fall
1989.

"A Bicycle. 1928.," "A Window On The Quai Voltaire. 1928.," "At The
Group Show. 1929.," "Rue Des Ursins. 1931.," "The Tuileries in the
Afternoon. 1963." in *Poetry Canada Review,* Vol. 10, No. 2, Summer
1989.

"Rue des Ursins. 1931." & "Medici Fountain. 1928." in *Grain,* Vol. XVI /
no. 4, 1988.

"At The Group Show. 1929." in *NeWest Review,* Oct. / Nov. 1988.

"Pont Marie at Night. 1963." in *Ice River* 3, Vol. 2 no. 1, 1988.

"Street Sweeper. 1923." in *Freelance,* Vol. XVIII no. 1, 1988.

"Tub Bath. Hospital For Sick Children. 1915." in *Freelance,* Vol. XVIII
no. 2, 1988.

Other poems from *Transient Light* are forthcoming in: *The Fiddlehead,
Rchaeology, Briarpatch, Rampike, Dandelion, Wascana Review,* and
Prism International.

Permissions

Afterword

Thank you to friends whose perceptive reading and comments on these poems, at various stages of the writing, were invaluable: Laureen Marchand, Gerry Shikatani, Richard Truhlar, and bp Nichol. Also thanks for occasional feedback from Anne Szumigalski, Ron Clark, Martha Gould, Susan Andrews Grace, and Paul Dutton.

I deeply appreciate the support and commitment of my publishers Beverley and Donald Daurio, and the astuteness of Beverley Daurio's editorial pencil.

Time and money are important, too. I am grateful for the support of: the Canada Council; the Saskatchewan Arts Board; the Saskatchewan Writers Guild Writers and Artists Colony Program; the Ontario Arts Council Writers Reserve Program; and finally the 1987-88 Weyburn Writer-In-Residence program sponsored by the Weyburn Public Library, the Saskatchewan Writers Guild, and Saskatchewan Parks Recreation & Culture.

These poems were written and revised between the summer of 1986 and the winter of 1989, in: Saskatchewan, at Saskatoon, Weyburn, St. Peter's Abbey in Muenster, and the Emma Lake Art Camp; and in Toronto, and Paris, France.

– Steven Smith

"a moment ago
the light was perfect"

Sharon Thesen

Other fine books from The Mercury Press (an imprint of Aya Press)

SKY – A Poem in Four Pieces by Libby Scheier
Order in the Universe and Other Stories by Veronica Ross
Directions for an Opened Body, Stories by Kenneth Harvey
Hard Times: An Anthology of New Fiction (Diamond, Jones,
    di Michele, Dutton, Shikatani, Ross, et al.)
Love and Hunger: An Anthology of New Fiction,
    Beverley Daurio, Editor (Atwood, McFadden, Jirgens, Truhlar, et al.)
With WK in the Workshop: A Memoir of William Kurelek
    by Brian Dedora
Poetry Markets for Canadians, James Deahl, Editor
    (with the League of Canadian Poets)
The Blue House by Lesley McAllister
Figures in Paper Time by Richard Truhlar
Ink & Strawberries: An Anthology of Quebec Women's Fiction (Blais,
    Brossard, Théoret, et al.)
1988: Selected Poems & Texts, 1973-88 by Gerry Shikatani

Please write for our complete catalogue:

The Mercury Press
(an imprint of Aya Press)
Box 446
Stratford, Ontario
Canada
N5A 6T3